quotes ,,

A companion guide of quotes to the Award Winning Book:

Show Up Be Bold Play Big: 33 Strategies for Outrageous Success and Lasting Happiness.

I love quotes.

I've loved quotes since I was a little girl. The power that just a few short words can carry is astonishing. They can change a mood or set you on a life changing path. Quotes inspire me. They encourage me. They remind me of things I need to know. It seems like I find myself spouting off one quote or another almost every single day. I've collected them for years – some filed neatly in organized files and some jotted down on post-it notes or napkins. But as I perused through my collection I came to the realization that words are to be shared – and I decided to compile them into one big glorious work. They mean a great deal to me. As I look them over I am reminded that these words have carried me through the highs and lows of an abundant life and the successes and pitfalls of my business ventures. They shaped my thinking and helped form my philosophies on life and business. They are a road map to my core philosophy for living: Show UP, Be BOLD, Play BIG.

I hope this little companion book to my most recent book, *Show Up, Be Bold, Play Big* will inspire and encourage you. I'm a firm believer that we are presented with exactly what we need to hear so I urge you to use 'Reading Roulette' – just flip open to a page and know whatever you find there is exactly meant for you in that moment!

Big Love,

Kim

Show UP

To show up is to be present to each moment and then to make decisions and choices from that place of total awareness. To be present in your life means to see the wonder in every moment. To be awake to possibilities. To see things most people miss when just going through the motions. When you are fully present, life becomes magical!

Here's to the moment!

If you miss the present moment, you miss your appointment with life.

Thich Nhat Hanh (1926 -)
Vietnamese scholar, activist & Buddhist monk

Life is all memory, except for the one present moment that goes by you so quickly you hardly catch it going.

Tennessee Williams (1911 – 1983)
American playwright

80% of all success is showing up.

Woody Allen (1935 -)
American screenwriter, director, author, actor & playwright

Wake up and Pay Attention

If you want be somebody, if you want to go somewhere, you better wake up and pay attention.

Sister Mary Clarence
in the film Sister Act (1992),
Lyricists Valeria Andrews and Ryan Toby

Luck is largely a matter of paying attention.

Susan M. Dodd
American author

The sleeping fox catches no poultry.

Benjamin Franklin (1706 – 1790)
American statesman and scientist

If I have ever made any valuable discoveries, it has been owing more to patient attention than to any other talent.

Isaac Newton (1643–1727)
English mathematician and physicist

Yesterday is gone. Tomorrow has not yet come. We have only today. Let us begin.

Mother Teresa (1910–1997)
*Albanian missionary &
Nobel Peace Prize winner*

Think Long, Think Wrong

The thing that cowardice fears most is decision.

Soren Kierkegaard (1813 – 1855)
Danish philosopher and writer

It's better to be boldly decisive and risk being wrong than to agonize at length and be right too late.

Unknown

You can't make progress without making decisions.

Jim Rohn (1930 – 2009)
American speaker, author & entrepreneur

The greatest advantage a man of mediocre talent can have over one of great genius is the ability to make decisions and act upon them.

O.A. Battista (1917 – 1995)
Canadian chemist and author

The risk of a wrong decision is preferable to the terror of indecision.

Maimonides (1135-1204)
Spanish Philosopher

Do it Now....
Then Do it Again

It is better to take many small steps in the right direction than to make a great leap forward only to stumble backward.

Proverb

Action may not always bring happiness, but there is no happiness without action.

Benjamin Disraeli (1804 – 1881)
British Prime Minister and Novelist

There are risks and costs of a program of action. But they are far less than the long-range risks and costs of comfortable inaction.

John F Kennedy (1917 – 1963)
35th President of the United States

What saves a man is to take a step. Then another step.

Antoine de Saint-Exupery (1900 – 1944)
French aviator and writer

Even if you're on the right track you'll get run over if you just sit there.

Will Rogers (1879 – 1935)
American cowboy and performer

Monitor and Adjust

I can't change the direction of the wind, but I can adjust my sails to always reach my destination.

Jimmy Dean (1928 – 2010)
American country music singer

When it is obvious the goals cannot be reached, don't adjust the goals, adjust the action steps.

Confucius (551 – 479 BC)
Chinese philosopher

The most serious mistakes are not being made as a result of wrong answers. The truly dangerous thing is asking the wrong question.

Peter Drucker (1909 – 2005)
Management Theorist and recipient of Presidential Medal of Freedom

If you live the questions, life will move you into the answers.

Deepak Chopra (1947)
Indian-American author and holistic health guru

Whosoever desires constant success must change his conduct with the times.

Niccolo Machiavelli (1469 – 1527)
Italian historian, philosopher and writer

Eliminate Distractions

By prevailing over all obstacles and distractions, one may unfailingly arrive at his chosen goal or destination.

Christopher Columbus (1451 – 1506)
Italian born Spanish navigator

Concentrate all your thoughts upon the work at hand. The suns' rays do not burn until brought to a focus.

Alexander Graham Bell (1847 – 1922)
Scottish scientist and inventor credited with inventing the telephone

Lack of direction, not lack of time, is the problem. We all have twenty-four hours a day.

Zig Ziglar (1926 – 2012)
American motivational speaker and author

You cannot eat every tadpole and frog in the pond, but you can eat the biggest and ugliest one, and that will be enough, at least for the time being.

Brian Tracy (1944 -)
American motivational speaker and author

The ability to apply your mind steadily and exclusively to one subject at a time is a mark of superior power and essential to really great achievement.

Grenville Kleiser, (1868 – 1935)
North American author

Look, Listen and Learn

A rock pile ceases to be a rock pile the moment a single man contemplates it, bearing within him the image of a cathedral.

Antoine de Saint-Exupery (1900 – 1944)
French aviator, poet and aristocrat

It is the province of knowledge to speak, and it is the privilege of wisdom to listen.

Oliver Wendell Holmes (1809 – 1894)
American physician, poet and professor

Whenever you are asked if you can do a job, tell 'em, Certainly I can! – and then get busy and find out how to do it!

Theodore Roosevelt (1858 – 1919)
26th President of the USA

Opportunities are often things you haven't noticed the first time around.

Catherine Deneuve (1943 -)
French actress

We don't know who discovered water, but we know it wasn't the fish.

Marshall McLuhan (1911 – 1980)
Canadian writer and social reformer

Yes, Yes and Yes

At the side of the everlasting why, is a yes, and a yes, and a yes.

E. M. Forster (1879 – 1970)
English novelist

Say yes and you'll figure it out afterwards.

Tina Fey (1970 -)
American actress, writer, producer and funny, funny lady

I imagine that yes is the only living thing.

e e cummings (1894 – 1962)
American poet and playwright

When you say "Yes' to others, make sure you are not saying 'No' to yourself.

Paolo Coehlo (1947 -)
Brazilian lyricist and novelist

Learn to say 'no' to the good so you can say 'yes' to the best.

John C. Maxwell (1947 -)
American author, speaker and pastor

Get Grand with Your Goals

Nothing can stop the man with the right mental attitude from achieving his goal; nothing on earth can help the man with the wrong mental attitude.

Thomas Jefferson (1743 – 1826)
3rd President of the USA

The word impossible is not in my dictionary.

Napoleon Bonaparte (1769 – 1821)
French military and political leader

Far better it is to dare mighty things, to win glorious triumphs, even though checkered by failure, than to take rank with those poor spirits who neither enjoy much nor suffer much, because they live in the gray twilight that knows not victory nor defeat.

Theodore Roosevelt (1858 – 1919)
26th President of the USA

To tend, unfailingly, unflinchingly, towards a goal, is the secret of success.

Anna Pavlova (1881 – 1931)
Russian ballerina

Show Me the Money Baby

Most people have no idea of the giant capacity we can immediately command when we focus all our resources on mastering a single area of our lives.

Tony Robbins (1960 –)
American self-help author and motivational speaker

Don't mistake activity with achievement.

John Wooden (1910 – 2010)
American basketball player and coach

Life is not easy for any of us. But what of that? We must have perseverance.

Marie Curie (1867 – 1934)
French physicist and chemist, two-time Nobel Prize winner

Beware lest you lose the substance by grasping at the shadow.

Aesop (620 – 564 BC)
Ancient Greek story teller

Risk more than others think is safe. Care more than others think is wise. Dream more than others think is practical. Expect more than others think is possible.

Claude Bissell (1916 – 2000)
Canadian author and educator

Get Over It

As long as you make an identity for yourself out of pain, you cannot be free of it.

Eckhart Tolle (1948 –)
German author on spirituality

We are not permitted to choose the frame of our destiny. But what we put into it is ours.

Dag Hammarskjold (1905 – 1961)
Swedish diplomat and Nobel Prize winner

The strongest oak of the forest is not the one that is protected from the storm and hidden from the sun. It's the one that stands in the open where it is compelled to struggle for its existence against the winds and rains and the scorching sun.

Napoleon Hill (1883 – 1970)
American author on personal success

The harder the conflict, the more glorious the triumph.

Thomas Paine (1737–1809)
American political theorist & writer

If there is no struggle, there is no progress.

Frederick Douglass (1818 – 1895)
American civil rights leader

Always Be Learning

Live as if you were to die tomorrow. Learn as if you were to live forever.

Mahatma Gandhi (1869 – 1948)
Indian freedom seeker who promoted nonviolent civil disobedience

The more I read, the more I acquire, the more certain I am that I know nothing.

Voltaire (1694 – 1778)
French enlightenment writer, historian and philosopher

The more that you read,
the more things you will know.
The more that you learn,
the more places you'll go.

Dr. Seuss (1904 – 1991)
American writer, poet and cartoonist

Education is the ability to
listen to almost anything
without losing your temper
or your self-confidence.

Robert Frost (1874 – 1963)
American poet

He who knows most,
knows how little he knows.

Thomas Jefferson (1743 – 1826)
3rd President of the USA

Be **BOLD**

To be bold is really just about being the very best and brightest you that you can possibly be. It's an approach to living life to the fullest so you can have what your heart desires. In business it's about standing out from the crowd. It's about separating yourself from everyone else out there. In life, it's about standing up for the only you there will ever be.

Stand up, stand out and be bold!

Let us endeavor so to live that when we come to die even the undertaker will be sorry.

Mark Twain (1835 – 1910)
American writer

Whatever you do, or dream you can, begin it. Boldness has genius and power and magic in it.

Johann Wolfgang von Goethe (1749 – 1832)
German writer and politician

Fortune befriends the bold.

Emily Dickinson (1830 – 1886)
American poet

Be Authentic

Be yourself.
Everyone else is taken.

Oscar Wilde (1854 – 1900)
Irish writer and poet

Have the courage to follow your heart and intuition. They somehow already know what you truly want to become. Everything else is secondary.

Steve Jobs (1955 – 2011)
Co-founder of Apple

To be nobody-but-yourself –
in a world which is doing its
best, night and day, to make
you everybody but yourself –
means to fight the hardest
battle which any human being
can fight, and never stop fighting.

e e cummings (1894 – 1962)
*American poet, painter, author
and playwright*

The privilege of a lifetime is to
become who you truly are.

Carl Jung (1875 – 1961)
Swiss psychiatrist

Whatever games are played
with us, we must play no
games with ourselves.

Ralph Waldo Emerson (1803 – 1882)
American writer and Transcendentalist

Be Different

In order to be irreplaceable one mush always be different.

Coco Chanel (1883 – 1971)
French fashion designer

Don't bend; don't water it down; don't try to make it logical; don't edit your own soul according to the fashion. Rather, follow your most intense obsessions mercilessly.

Franz Kafka (1883 – 1924)
German novelist

Here's to the crazy ones.
The misfits. The rebels.
The troublemakers. The round
pegs in the square holes. The
ones who see things differently.
They're not fond of rules.
And they have no respect for the
status quo. You can quote them,
disagree with them, glorify or vilify
them. About the only thing you
can't do is ignore them. Because
they change things. They push the
human race forward. And while
some may see them as the crazy
ones, we see genius. Because the
people who are crazy enough to
think they can change the world,
are the ones who do.

Apple, Inc. as created by
TBWA\Chiat\Day Agency

Be Fearless

Avoiding danger is no safer in the long run than outright exposure. The fearful are caught as often as the bold.

Helen Keller (1880 – 1968)
American author, political activist and lecturer

Whatever there be of progress in life comes not through adaptation but through daring.

Henry Miller (1891 – 1980)
American author

Never stop because you are afraid - you are never so likely to be wrong.

Fridtjof Nansen (1861 – 1930)
Norwegian explorer, Nobel Peace Prize winner

Valor grows by daring, fear by holding back.

Publilius Syrus
1st Century BC writer of moral maxims

It is better to err on the side of daring than the side of caution.

Alvin Toffler (1928 –)
American writer and futurist

Daring ideas are like chessmen moving forward; they may be beaten, but they may start a winning game.

Johann Wolfgang von Goethe (1749 – 1832)
German writer and politician

Be Optimistic

The last of the human freedoms – to choose one's attitude in any given set of circumstances, to choose one's own way.

Viktor Frankl (1905 – 1997)
Austrian neurologist and psychiatrist

"What day is it?"
"It's today," squeaked Piglet.
"My favorite day," said Pooh.

A.A. Milne (1882 – 1956)
English author and creator of Winnie the Pooh

The optimist sees the rose and not its thorns; the pessimist stares at the thorns, oblivious of the rose.

Kahlil Gibran, (1883 – 1931)
Lebanese writer and philosopher

Don't cry because it's over, smile because it happened.

Dr. Seuss (1904 – 1991)
American writer, poet and cartoonist

A pessimist sees the difficulty in every opportunity; an optimist sees the opportunity in every difficulty.

Winston Churchill (1874 – 1965)
British politician and statesman

Be Non-Judgmental

Everything that irritates us about others can lead us to an understanding of ourselves.

Carl Jung (1875 – 1961)
Swiss psychiatrist

We judge others by their behaviors. We judge ourselves by our intentions.

Ian Percy (1880 – 1930)
8th Duke of Northumberland

Judge not lest ye
be judged.

Matthew 7:1
The Bible, King James Version

If you judge people, you
have no time to love them.

Mother Teresa (1910 – 1997)
Albanian missionary &
Nobel Peace Prize winner

Everybody is a genius.
But if you judge a fish by its
ability to climb a tree, it will
live its whole life believing
that it is stupid.

Albert Einstein (1879 – 1955)
German-born theoretical physicist and really
smart guy

Be Aware of
the Lesson

One day in retrospect the years of struggle will strike you as the most beautiful.

Sigmund Freud (1856 – 1939)
Austrian psychiatrist

The aim of life is to live, and to live means to be aware, joyously, drunkenly, serenely, divinely aware.

Henry Miller (1891 – 1980)
American writer

Smooth seas do not make skillful sailors.

African Proverb

Things turn out best for people who make the best of the way things turn out.

Art Linkletter (1912 – 2010)
Canadian-born American radio and television personality

Let us not look back in anger, nor forward in fear, but around us in awareness.

James Thurber (1894 – 1961)
American author and cartoonist

Be in Right Relationship

In any moment of decision, the best thing you can do is the right thing, the next best thing is the wrong thing, and the worst thing you can do is nothing.

Theodore Roosevelt (1858 – 1919)
26th President of the USA

The time is always right to do what is right.

Martin Luther King Jr. (1929 – 1968)
American clergyman and Civil Rights activist

Always do right. This will gratify some people, and astonish the rest.

Mark Twain (1835 – 1910)
American writer

There is nothing either good or bad except that thinking makes it so.

Shakespeare (1564 – 1616)
English poet and playwright

People underestimate their capacity for change. There is never a right time to do a difficult thing.

John Porter (1790 – 1874)
New York politician

Be Excessive

If you rarely give a little more, should you really expect to get a little more?

Sam Parker
Co-founder of JustSell

Don't live down to expectations. Go out there and do something remarkable.

Wendy Wasserstein (1950 – 2006)
American playwright

Make happy those
who are near, and those
who are far will come.

Chinese proverb

Formula for success: under
promise and over deliver.

Tom Peters (1942)
American business writer

We make a living by what
we get. We make a life by
what we give.

Winston Churchill (1874 – 1965)
British politician and statesman

Always do more than is
required of you.

George Patton (1885 – 1945)
United States Army General

Be Risky, Not Reckless

The fishermen know that the sea is dangerous and the storm terrible, but they have never found those dangers sufficient reason for remaining ashore.

Vincent van Gogh (1853 – 1890)
Dutch painter

Progress always involves risk; you can't steal second base and keep your foot on first base.

Frederick Wilcox (1904 – 1979)
American literary critic

Only those who risk going too far can possibly find out how far they can go.

T.S. Eliot (1888 – 1965)
American-born British playwright and literary critic

And the trouble is, if you don't risk anything, you risk more.

Erica Jong (1942 -)
American writer and feminist

I've been terrified every moment of my life and I've never let it keep me from doing a single thing that I wanted to do.

Georgia O'Keeffe (1887 – 1986)
American artist

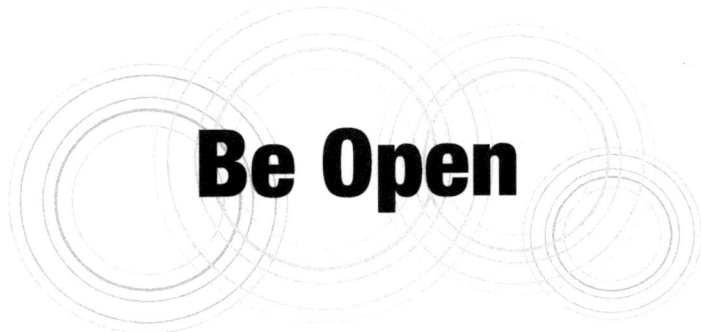

Be Open

The walls we build around us to keep out the sadness also keep out the joy.

Jim Rohn (1930 – 2009)
American speaker, author & entrepreneur

Most of our assumptions have outlived their uselessness.

Marshall McLuhan (1911 – 1980)
Canadian philosopher and scholar

It's wonderful to have
a beginner's mind.

Steve Jobs (1955 – 2011)
Co-founder of Apple

As for the future, your
task is not to foresee it,
but to enable it.

Antoine de Saint-Exupery (1900 – 1944)
French aviator and writer

It'll all be okay in the end.
If it's not okay, it's not the end.

John Lennon (1940 – 1980)
English musician, singer and songwriter

What would life be if
we had no courage to
attempt anything?

Vincent van Gogh (1853 – 1890)
Dutch painter

Be Still

Man has to learn to seek first the kingdom of heaven, the place of stillness and quiet at the highest level of which he is capable, and then the heavenly influences can pour into him, recreate him, recreate him and use him for the salvation of mankind.

White Eagle
Pawnee Chief

Don't just do something, sit there.

Sylvia Boorstein
Meditation teacher

If you want others to follow, learn to be alone with your thoughts.

William Deresiewicz (1964 –)
American writer and literary critic

The quieter you become, the more you can hear.

Baba Ram Dass (1931 –)
American spiritual teacher

The intuitive mind is a sacred gift and the rational mind is a faithful servant. We have created a society that honors the servant and has forgotten the gift.

Albert Einstein (1879 – 1955)
German-born theoretical physicist and really smart guy

Play BIG

Playing big is about living life to the fullest. It's about not playing small to make anyone else comfortable, but being the biggest, best, most outrageous you! To go somewhere you've never gone, or to accomplish something that's bigger than you are, you have to think in certain ways and remember that you're here for greatness.

Go Play BIG!

Always bear in mind that your own resolution to succeed is more important than any other one thing.

Abraham Lincoln (1809 – 1865)
16th President of the USA

The master in the art of living makes little distinction between his work and his play, his labor and his leisure, his mind and his body, his information and his recreation, his love and his religion. He hardly knows which is which. He simply pursues his vision of excellence at whatever he does, leaving others to decide whether he is working or playing. To him he's always doing both.

James A. Michener (1907 – 1997)
American author

Love What You Do

Pleasure in the job puts perfection in the work.

Aristotle (384bc–322bc)
Greek philosopher, physician & scientist

Nothing is really work unless you would rather be doing something else.

James M. Barrie (1860 – 1937)
Dramatist and creator of Peter Pan

Nothing is so contagious as enthusiasm.

Edward George Bulwer-Lytton (1803 – 1873)
English politician and writer

There is no greater gift you can give or receive than to honor your calling. It's why you were born. And how you become most truly alive.

Oprah (1954 -)
American media proprietor, philanthropist and down-right amazing woman

Your work is to discover your world and then with all your heart give yourself to it.

Buddha, *Indian spiritual teacher*

Believe in [your business] more than anyone does. Passion is at the top of the list of the skills you need to excel.

Sam Walton (1918 – 1992)
American businessman and founder of Walmart

Dream Big

I learned this, at least, by my experiment: that if one advances confidently in the direction of his dreams, and endeavors to live the life which he has imagined, he will meet with a success unexpected in common hours.

Henry David Thoreau (1817 – 1862)
American author, poet and philosopher

All men of action
are dreamers.

James Huneker (1857 – 1921)
American music writer and critic

The greatest human tempta-
tion is to settle for too little.

Thomas Merton (1915 – 1968)
Anglo-American Catholic writer,
mystic and monk

You are never too old to
set another goal or to
dream a new dream.

C.S. Lewis (1898 – 1963)
British scholar and novelist

Who wants a dream
that's near-fetched?

Howard Schultz (1953 -)
American businessman and
Chairman of Starbucks

Act As If

Act as if you were already happy and that will tend to make you happy.

Dale Carnegie (1888 – 1955)
American lecturer and author

An attitude of positive expectation is the mark of the superior personality.

Brian Tracy (1944 -)
American motivational speaker and author

I dwell in possibility.

Emily Dickinson (1830 – 1886)
American poet

If you want quality, act as if you already have it. If you want to be courageous, act as if you were – and as you act and persevere in acting, so you tend to become.

Norman Vincent Peale (1898 – 1993)
American minister and author

Act as if what you do makes a difference. It does.

William James (1842 – 1910)
American psychologist and philosopher

See it for Yourself

Beware what you set your heart upon for surely it shall be yours.

Ralph Waldo Emerson (1803–1882)
American writer and Transcendentalist

Imagination is the beginning of creation. You imagine what you desire, you will what you imagine, and at last, you create what you will.

George Bernard Shaw (1856 – 1950)
Irish playwright

There are only two ways to live your life. One is though nothing is a miracle. The other is as though everything is a miracle.

Albert Einstein (1879 – 1955)
German-born theoretical physicist and really smart guy

You can't win any game unless you are ready to win.

Connie Mack (1862 – 1956)
American professional baseball player, manager and team owner

The secret of making something work in your lives is, first of all, the deep desire to make it work; then the faith and belief that it can work; then to hold that clear definite vision in your consciousness and see it working out step by step, without one doubt or disbelief.

Eileen Caddy (1917 – 2006)
Scottish writer and spiritual leader

Celebrate All Successes and Failures

Ever tried. Ever failed.
No matter. Try again.
Fail again. Fail better.

Samuel Beckett (1906 – 1989)
Irish avant-garde novelist and playwright

Life has meaning only in the struggle. Triumph or defeat is in the hands of the gods. So let us celebrate the struggle.

Swahili Warrior Song

Never regret. If it's good, it's wonderful. If it's bad, it's experience.

Victoria Holt (1906 – 1993)
British writer

There is nothing either good or bad except that thinking makes it so.

William Shakespeare (1564 – 1616)
English poet and playwright

Mistakes are part of the dues one pays for a full life.

Sophia Loren (1934 -)
Italian actress

Whenever you fall, pick up something.

Oswald Theodore Avery (1877 – 1955)
Canadian-born American physician and medical researcher

Quit the Blame Game

Life is a series of near misses. But a lot of what we ascribe to luck is not luck at all. It's seizing the day and accepting responsibility for your future.

Howard Schultz (1953 -)
American businessman and Chairman of Starbucks

I attribute my success to this: I never gave or took an excuse.

Florence Nightingale (1820–1910)
English pioneer of modern nursing

Ninety-nine percent of all failures come from people who have a habit of making excuses.

George Washington Carver (1864 – 1943)
American scientist, educator and former slave

People are always blaming their circumstances for what they are. I don't believe in circumstances. The people who get on in this world are the people who get up and look for the circumstances they want, and if they can't find them, make them.

George Bernard Shaw (1856 – 1950)
Irish playwright

Master Your Thoughts

He who cannot change the very fabric of his thought will never be able to change reality, and will never, therefore, make any progress.

Anwar el-Sadat (1918 – 1981)
Egyptian president and winner of the Nobel Peace Prize

A wise man changes his mind, a fool never.

Spanish proverb

A man is but the product of his thoughts – what he thinks, he becomes.

Mahatma Gandhi (1869 – 1948)
Indian philosopher

You conceive your world in your mind and then create it with your hands.

Chris Widener (1963 -)
American politician

Great men are those who see that thoughts rule the world.

Ralph Waldo Emerson (1803–1882)
American writer and Transcendentalist

Have Some Fun

As long as you're having fun, that's the key. The moment it becomes a grind, it's over.

Barry Gibb (1946 -)
English musician, singer and songwriter

People rarely succeed unless they have fun in what they are doing.

Dale Carnegie (1888 – 1955)
American lecturer and author

Live and work but do not
forget to play, to have fun in
life and really enjoy it.

Eileen Caddy (1917 – 2006)
Scottish writer and spiritual leader

If it's not fun,
I'm not interested.

Kim Hodous (1963 -)
Author, speaker and lover of life

The truest greatness lies
in being kind, the truest
wisdom in a happy mind.

Ella Wheeler Wilcox (1850 – 1919)
American author and poet

Allow Others to Help You

Many hands and hearts and minds generally contribute to anyone's notable achievements.

Walt Disney (1901 – 1966)
American motion-picture producer and pioneer of animated cartoon films

As iron sharpens iron, so one person sharpens another.

Proverbs 27:17
The Bible, New International Version

No degree of knowledge attainable by man is able to set him above the want of hourly assistance.

Samuel Johnson (1709 – 1784)
English poet, essayist and moralist

The love we give away is the only love we keep.

Elbert Hubbard (1856 – 1915)
American writer, artist and philosopher

It is one of the most beautiful compensations of life that no man can sincerely try to help another, without helping himself.

John P. Webster (1580 – 1634)
English Jacobean dramatist

Give Back

You only have what you give. It's by spending yourself that you become rich.

Isabel Allende (1942 -)
Chilean-American novelist

If America is the pursuit of happiness, the best way to pursue happiness is to help other people.

George Lucas (1944 -)
American film director, producer and creator of Star Wars

Nothing liberates our greatness like the desire to help, the desire to serve.

Marianne Williamson (1952 -)
Spiritual activist and author

I feel the greatest reward for doing is the opportunity to do more.

Jonas Salk (1914 – 1995)
American medical researcher and developer of the polio vaccine

Therefore encourage one another and build each other up.

1 Thessalonians 5:11
The Bible, New International Version

Be Grateful for Everything, All the Time

Cultivate the habit of being grateful for every good thing that comes to you, and to give thanks continuously. And because all things have contributed to your advancement, you should include all things in your gratitude.

Ralph Waldo Emerson (1803–1882)
American writer and Transcendentalist

Who does not thank for little will not thank for much.

Estonian Proverb

Trade your expectation for appreciation and the world changes instantly.

Tony Robbins (1960 -)
American self-help author and motivational speaker

Feeling gratitude and not expressing it is like wrapping a present and not giving it.

William Arthur Ward (1921 – 1994)
American author and teacher

He is a wise man who does not grieve for the things which he has not, but rejoices for those which he has.

Epictetus (55 AD – 135 AD)
Greek sage and philosopher

Whether you're looking to enhance the experience of implementing my *33 Strategies for Outrageous Success and Lasting Happiness from Show UP Be Bold Play Big* or just looking for a bit of daily inspiration, I hope these quotes that have meant so much to me will bring the same to you! And on our collective journey to more abundant lives and bigger successes, I have one final thought to share:

It doesn't matter where you start. What matters is where you're going.

Kim Hodous

Now get going! And may these quotes provide inspiration and comfort along the way.

Kim Hodous knows about success in the real world. She took a kitchen table hobby and turned it into a seven-figure business – despite being a former high-school history teacher with zero business experience. She combines the lessons she learned along the way with a fresh perspective on life to give an original and inspirational slant on success, happiness, health and staying motivated so you can live life to the fullest.

To put Kim in a box is impossible. But to try and sum her up, here goes: She inspires thousands of people each year. She speaks for hundreds of organizations & companies annually. She's spoken to just about every major industry and is requested by Fortune 100 Companies. She's nationally known on the topics of work/life balance, leadership, communication, networking (the old fashioned way – face-to-face), productivity and getting more of what you want out of life. She's also a Best-Selling Author, an Award-Winning Business Woman, a Yoga Instructor, and the mother of five!

Bottom line: Get Ready! Kim is a fearless, no-nonsense speaker with a unique perspective and strategies that actually work in the real world.

To Schedule Kim to Speak At your Next Event:
888-784-7489 • www.kimhodous.com

www.ingramcontent.com/pod-product-compliance
Lightning Source LLC
LaVergne TN
LVHW020440250425
809387LV00007B/20